The Underground Railroad: Life on the Road to Freedom

D1463033

Edited and introduced by
Pat Perrin

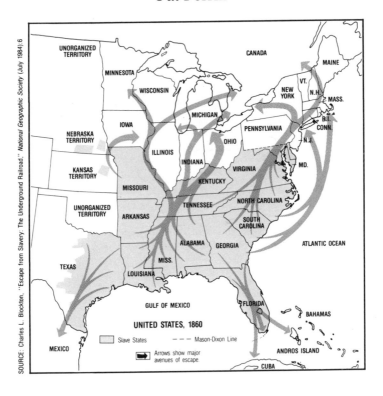

SOURCE: Charles L. Blockton, "Escape from Slavery: The Underground Railroad," *National Geographic Society* (July 1984):6

UNORGANIZED TERRITORY

MINNESOTA

WISCONSIN

CANADA

MAINE

VT.

N.H.

MASS.

NEW YORK

MICHIGAN

IOWA

NEBRASKA TERRITORY

ILLINOIS

INDIANA

OHIO

PENNSYLVANIA

R.I.

CONN.

N.J.

MD.

KANSAS TERRITORY

MISSOURI

KENTUCKY

VIRGINIA

UNORGANIZED TERRITORY

ARKANSAS

TENNESSEE

NORTH CAROLINA

SOUTH CAROLINA

ALABAMA

GEORGIA

ATLANTIC OCEAN

TEXAS

MISS.

LOUISIANA

GULF OF MEXICO

UNITED STATES, 1860

Slave States

Mason-Dixon Line

Arrows show major avenues of escape.

MEXICO

FLORIDA

BAHAMAS

ANDROS ISLAND

CUBA

Discovery Enterprises, Ltd.
Carlisle, Massachusetts

Second Edition © Discovery Enterprises, Ltd., Carlisle, MA 1999

First Edition © Discovery Enterprises, Ltd., Carlisle, MA 1995

ISBN 1-57960-051-4 paperback edition
Library of Congress Catalog Card Number 99-62411

10 9 8 7 6 5 4 3 2 1

Printed in the United States of America

Subject Reference Guide:

The Underground Railroad: Life on the Road to Freedom
Edited and Introduced by Pat Perrin

Underground Railroad — U. S. History

Abolition of Slavery

Photos/Illustrations:

Cover illustration: A poor fugitive is from one of the stereotype cuts used on handbills offering rewards for runaway slaves.

Other illustrations are credited where they appear in the text.

Table of Contents

Introduction: Building a Railroad 5
by Pat Perrin

Making the Decision 7
Dreaming of Liberty 7
Fearing to Flee 8
Leaving Friends Behind 10
Seeing What I Was Coming To 10
Separating Families 11
Searching for Loved Ones 13
Buying Freedom 14
Running Away from the White House 14

Moving Words 17
David Walker's Appeal 18
William Lloyd Garrison's Liberator 20
The Fugitive Slave Acts 21
Harriet Beecher Stowe's Uncle Tom's Cabin 25

Signs and Songs to Follow 26
Spirituals 27

Going in Disguise 31
Anna Maria Weems as a Male 31
William and Ellen Craft as Master and Slave 32
Frederick Douglass as a Sailor 35
Henry Brown as a Package 40

Stories of the Long Hard Trip 43
Help along the Way 44
The Fourth Try for Freedom 50
Troubles on The Road 55
The Fourth Try for Freedom 50

Those Who Helped 57

Moses Leads the Way 58

Levi Coffin's Railroad Station 63

Epilogue 65

Suggested Further Reading 66

Introduction:
Building a Railroad

by Pat Perrin

I was now about twelve years old, and the thought of being a slave for life began to bear heavily upon my heart.

— Frederick Douglass
Narrative of the Life of Frederick Douglass,
An American Slave, Written by Himself

The literate, highly intelligent, Douglass did escape from bondage, and he became one of the most famous American orators of his day. Some of his story is included here, along with the stories of many others who would settle for nothing less than freedom. Many of the documents quoted are primary sources; some are secondary sources that were published in the nineteenth century.

The social system to which slaves were brought or born offered no release. A few masters allowed a few slaves to buy their own freedom, but that option was not open to most. And so they escaped on their own.

By the thousands, enslaved African Americans slipped away from imprisonment and headed north to the states where slavery was illegal. They went by every kind of transportation—wagons, boats, even trains —but most by far went on foot. Along the way, some people—both black and white—helped the fugitives by hiding them, signaling them when they could safely stop for the night in a particular location, and giving advice on the route to take. The helpers put themselves in the same danger as the fleeing slaves, and some were imprisoned for their actions. In the Northern cities, others helped the refugees find places to sleep and work.

Some who had fled enslavement returned to show others the way. Again and again, they risked losing what they had gained for themselves in order to help others be free.

In the early nineteenth-century, a loosely connected network of secret routes, hiding places, and helpers extended throughout fourteen Northern states and into Canada. It all became known as the Underground Railroad—"underground" because, of course, it was secret, hidden. According to one story, a master complained that his fleeing slave had disappeared without a trace, as if he had "gone off on some underground road." ("Aboard the UnderGround Railroad," National Park Service website: http://www.cr.nps.gov/nr/underground/)

At that time, trains were new, fast, and powerful. The term "railroad" no doubt expressed the hope that the escape route would be just as powerful in transporting refugees to freedom. The name also supplied a system of code words that could alert potential passengers when it was safe to travel. The following information appeared on the National Park Service Underground Railroad website: http://www.cr.nps.gov/nr/underground/.

> Similar to an actual railroad, the act of transporting the escaped slaves incorporated all the terms used during a railroad journey:
>
> - The routes from safe-house to safe-house (houses where the fugitive slaves were kept) were called 'lines'.
> - Stopping places were called 'stations'.
> - Those who aided fugitive slaves were known as 'conductors'.
> - In order to keep terms as clandestine as possible, the fugitive slaves were known as 'packages' or 'freight'.

Although the railroad was never formally organized, thousands of refugees traveled along its lines between 1830 and 1865. Estimates of those who reached freedom range from 40,000 to 100,000. No complete records were kept, and some of the routes and stations are still being discovered.

Making the Decision

The conditions under which slaves lived gave them plenty of reason to want to escape. (See Phyllis Raybin Emert, ed., Colonial Triangular Trade: An Economy Based on Human Misery, *Discovery Enterprises, 1995.) However most of the people who ran away simply wanted to be free. They were well aware that they faced many dangers if they tried to escape, but sometimes they could only imagine what those dangers might be.*

Dreaming of Liberty

Lewis Clarke was a Kentucky slave in the 1840s. After he made his escape, Clarke's memoirs became an important source of information for Harriet Beecher Stowe when she wrote her famous novel Uncle Tom's Cabin.

Source: Lewis Clarke in Harriet Beecher Stowe, *The Key to Uncle Tom's Cabin,* Boston, 1854, pp. 21-22. Found in William Loren Katz, *Eyewitness: A Living Documentary of the African American Contribution to American History*, New York: Simon and Schuster, 1995, p. 127.

I had long thought and dreamed of LIBERTY; I was now determined to make an effort to gain it. No tongue can tell the doubt, the perplexities, the anxiety, which a slave feels when making up his mind upon this subject. If he makes an effort and is not successful, he must be laughed at by his fellows, he will be beaten unmercifully by the master, and then watched and used the harder for it all his life.

And then, if he gets away, who, what, will he find? He is ignorant of the world. All the white part of mankind that he has ever seen are enemies to him and all his kindred. How can he venture where none but white faces shall greet him?

The master tells him that abolitionists[1] decoy slaves off into the free states to catch them and sell them to Louisiana or Mississippi; and, if he goes to Canada, the British will put him in a mine under ground, with both eyes put out, for life. How does he know what or whom to believe? A horror of great darkness comes upon him, as he thinks over what might befall him. Long, very long time did I think of escaping before I made the effort.

At length the report was started that I was to be sold for Louisiana. Then I thought it was time to act. My mind was made up.

Fearing to Flee

Frederick Douglass also knew that "the odds were fearful" against success. In his autobiography he described the fears that confronted those who contemplated escape. Douglass, like Adams (p. 10), went to freedom anyway.

Source: Frederick Douglass, *Narrative of the Life of Frederick Douglass, An American Slave, Written by Himself.* Boston: 1845; New York: Doubleday & Co., 1963, pp. 84-86.

Our path was beset with the greatest obstacles; and if we succeeded in gaining the end of it, our right to be free was yet questionable—we were yet liable to be returned to bondage. We could see no spot, this side of the ocean, where we could be free. We knew nothing about Canada. Our knowledge of the north did not extend farther than New York; and to go there, and be forever harassed with the frightful liability of being returned to slavery—with the certainty of

---

[1] Those who favored ending slavery called themselves Abolitionists. See the chapter entitled "Those Who Helped."

being treated tenfold worse than before—the thought was truly a horrible one, and one which it was not easy to overcome. The case sometimes stood thus: At every gate through which we were to pass, we saw a watchman—at every ferry a guard—on every bridge a sentinel—and in every wood a patrol. We were hemmed in on every side. Here were the difficulties, real or imagined—the good to be sought and the evil to be shunned. On the one hand, there stood slavery, a stern reality, glaring frightfully upon us,—its robes already crimsoned with the blood of millions and even now feasting itself greedily upon our own flesh. On the other hand, away back in the dim distance, under the flickering light of the north star, behind some craggy hill or snow-covered mountain, stood a doubtful freedom—half frozen—beckoning us to come and share its hospitality. This in itself was sometimes enough to stagger us; but when we permitted ourselves to survey the road, we were frequently appalled. Upon either side we saw grim death, assuming the most horrid shapes. Now it was starvation, causing us to eat our own flesh;—now we were contending with the waves, and were drowned;—now we were overtaken, and torn to pieces by the fangs of the terrible bloodhound. We were stung by scorpions, chased by wild beasts, bitten by snakes, and finally, after having nearly reached the desired spot,—after swimming rivers, encountering wild beasts, sleeping in the woods, suffering hunger and nakedness,—we were overtaken by our pursuers, and, in our resistance, we were shot dead upon the spot.

Leaving Friends Behind

Douglass also described the pain of leaving others behind.

Source: Frederick Douglass, *op cit.,* pp. 104-105.

It is impossible for me to describe my feelings as the time of my contemplated start drew near. I had a number of warm-hearted friends in Baltimore,—friends that I loved almost as I did my life,—and the thought of being separated from them forever was painful beyond expression. It is my opinion that thousands would escape from slavery, who now remain, but for the strong cords of affection that bind them to their friends. The thought of leaving my friends was decidedly the most painful thought with which I had to contend. The love of them was my tender point, and shook my decision more than all things else.

Seeing What I Was Coming To

In 1855, Boston educator and journalist Benjamin Drew collected and published narratives from among the estimated 30,000 fugitive slaves in Canada as A North-Side View of Slavery. *(See the chapter entitled "Moving Words.") The young James Adams told Drew that he had not yet been badly treated when he decided to escape, but he could see what was ahead of him.*

Source: James Adams, from Benjamin Drew, ed., *The Refugee: or Narratives of Fugitive Slaves in Canada Related by Themselves.* Boston, 1856.

I was raised in Virginia, about twenty miles above the mouth of the Big Kanawha. At the age of seventeen, I set out to seek freedom in company with Benjamin Harris, (who was a cousin of mine) . . . I was young, and they had not treated me very badly; but I had seen older men treated worse than a horse or a hog ought to be treated; so, seeing what I was coming to, I wished to get away. My father being overseer, I was not used so badly as some even younger than myself, who were kicked, cuffed, and whipped very badly for little or nothing.

....

I look upon slavery as the most disgusting system a man can live under. . . . Men who have never seen or felt slavery cannot realize it for the thing it is. If those who say that fugitives had better go back, were to go to the South and *see* slavery, they would never wish any slave to go back.

I have seen separations by sales, of husbands from wives, of parents from children,—if a man threatens to run away, he is sure to be sold. Ben's mother was sold down South —to New Orleans—when he was about twenty years old.

Separating Families

Thomas Hedgbeth was born free in Halifax, North Carolina, then moved to Indiana, and later to Canada. Although Hedgbeth was not a slave, he suffered from the prohibition about teaching African Americans to read or write. He told Drew, "My ignorance has had a very injurious effect on my prospects and success." Hedgbeth described the treatment of slaves, including of families.

Source: Benjamin Drew, ed., *The Refugee, op cit.,* pp. 276-280.

I have seen families put on the block and sold, some one way, some another way. I remember a family about two miles from me,—a father and mother and three children. Their master died, and they were sold. The father went one way, the mother another, with one child, and the other two children another way. I saw the sale—I was there—I went to buy hogs. The purchaser examined the persons of the slaves to see if they were sound,—if they were "good niggers." I was used to such things, but it made me feel bad to see it. The oldest was about ten or eleven years. It was hard upon them to be separated—they made lamentations about it. I never heard a white man at a sale express a wish that a family might be sold together.

Slaves were auctioned off to the highest bidder.

Searching for Loved Ones

Some enslaved people escaped in an effort to find lost loved ones. Since they did not leave the slave states, many of these were recaptured. Their owners published reward notices such as the following in Southern newspapers.

Source: Theodore Dwight Weld, *American Slavery As It Is. Testimony of a Thousand Witnesses* (New York, 1839), pp. 164-166. Found in William Loren Katz, *op cit.*, pp. 116–117.

Macon (Ga.) *Messenger*, November 23, 1837.

$25 Reward. —Ran away, a Negro man, named Cain. He was brought from Florida, and has a wife near Mariana, and probably will attempt to make his way there.

Richmond (Va.) *Compiler*, September 8, 1837.

Ran away from the subscriber, Ben. He ran off without any known cause, and I suppose he is aiming to go to his wife, who was carried from the neighborhood last winter.

Richmond (Va.) *Enquirer*, February 20, 1838.

Stop the Runaway!!!! —$25 Reward. Ran away from the Eagle Tavern, a Negro fellow named Nat. He is no doubt attempting to follow his wife, who was lately sold to a speculator named Redmond. The above reward will be paid by Mrs. Lucy M. Downman, of Sussex County, Va.

Savannah (Ga.) *Republican*, September 3, 1838.

$20 Reward for my Negro man Jim. —Jim is about 50 or 55 years of age. It is probable he will aim for Savannah, as he said he had children in that vicinity.

Lexington (Ky.) *Observer and Reporter*, September 28, 1838.

$50 Reward. —Ran away from the subscriber, a Negro girl, named Maria. She is of a copper color, between 13 and 14 years of age—bare headed and bare footed. She is small of her age— very sprightly and very likely. She stated she was going to see her mother at Maysville.

Buying Freedom

Even slaves who were not mistreated wanted to be free. Henry Blue was one of the few who was allowed to save money and to purchase his own freedom.

Source: Benjamin Drew, *op cit.,* pp. 276.

I learned the trade of a blacksmith in Kentucky. I should have been perfectly miserable to have had to work all my life for another man for nothing. As soon as I had arrived to years of discretion, I felt determined that I would not be a slave all my days. My master was a kind and honorable man; purchased no slaves himself: what he had, came by marriage. He used to say it was wrong to hold slaves, and a good many who hold them say the same. It's a habit—they mean, they say, to set them free at such a time, or such a time,—by and by they die, and the children hold on to the slaves.

Running Away from the White House

James Christian served the family of President Tyler in the White House and freely admitted that he had been treated kindly. But because he was a slave, Christian could not marry the free African American woman that he loved. Christian ran away and was later interviewed at the Philadelphia station of the Underground Railroad.

Source: William Still, *The Underground Rail Road,* Philadelphia, 1872, pp. 69-70. Found in William Loren Katz, *op cit.,* pp. 130-131.

"I have always been treated well; if I only have half as good times in the North as I have had in the South, I shall be perfectly satisfied. Any time I desired spending money, five or

House slaves were treated better than field slaves.
Above is a slave coachman.

ten dollars were no object.". . . with regard to food also, he had fared as well as heart could wish, with abundance of leisure time at his command. His deportment was certainly very refined and gentlemanly. . . . He had been to William and Mary's College in his younger days, to wait on young master James B. C. where, through the kindness of some of the students, he had picked up a trifling amount of book learning.

. . . On the death of the old Major [Christian, his owner] James fell into the hands of his son, judge Christian. . . . Subsequently he fell into the hands of one of the judge's sisters, Mrs. John Tyler (wife of ex-President Tyler), and then he became a member of the President's domestic household, was at the White House, under the President, from 1841 to 1845. . . .

"How did you like Mr. Tyler?" said an inquisitive member of the Vigilance Committee. "I didn't like Mr. Tyler much," was the reply. "Why?" again inquired the member of the Committee. "Because Mr. Tyler was a poor man. I never did like poor people. I didn't like his marrying into our family, who were considered very far Tyler's superiors." "On the plantation," he said, "Tyler was a very cross man, and treated the servants very cruelly; but the house servants were treated much better, owing to their having belonged to his wife, who protected them from persecution, as they had been favorite servants in her father's family." James estimated that "Tyler got about thirty-five thousand dollars and twenty-nine slaves, young, and old, by his wife."

Moving Words

Publications and speeches often helped turn thoughts of freedom into actions. Successful fugitives told or wrote their stories, which left many readers determined to help others escape. (Several fugitive slave narratives are included in upcoming chapters.) Journals and pamphlets also stirred a wide audience among the free and the enslaved. Even new laws passed to prohibit helping escaped slaves often provoked more escapes and brought more supporters into the conflict.

THE

ANTI-SLAVERY RECORD.

Vol. III. No. VII.   JULY, 1837.   Whole No. 31.

Cover illustration from The Anti-Slavery Record,
Vol. III, No. VII (July, 1837).

David Walker's Appeal

David Walker (1785–1830) was an educated, free black man who traveled throughout the South and saw slavery first-hand. He became an Abolitionist in Boston and often contributed to Freedom's Journal, an anti-slavery weekly. In the 1820s, Walker opened a store on the Boston waterfront where he sold used clothing to seamen. He hid copies of his Appeal for a slave revolt in the pockets of the garments, knowing that some would reach other used-clothes dealers in Southern ports. He also gave copies of the Appeal to sympathetic black seamen who could distribute them in the South.

The appearance of Walker's pamphlets aroused great alarm in the Southern states, leading to laws that prohibited Abolitionist literature and forbid slaves to learn to read and write. Walker was warned that his life was in danger, but he refused to flee to Canada. When his body was found near his shop, many believed he had been poisoned. Most antislavery leaders and free blacks rejected Walker's call for violence at this time, but his work drew considerable attention to the cause.

Source: Courtesy of the Museum of Afro American History, Boston, MA, from Margaret A. Drew and William S. Parsons, *The African Meeting House in Boston – A Sourcebook*, The Museum of Afro American History, 1990.

Walker is remembered . . . for a pamphlet that he published in 1829. Known as *Walker's Appeal,* the full title of the seventy-six page pamphlet was *Walker's Appeal, in Four Articles: Together with a Preamble, to the Coloured Citizens of the World, but in particular, and very expressly, to those in the United States of America, written in Boston, State of Massachusetts, September 28, 1829.* The four articles mentioned in the title address four separate issues: Article 1 deals with slavery and its evil consequences; Article 2, with the black's lack of education; Article 3 addresses the upholding of the slave system by the Christian ministry; and Article 4 is concerned with the colonization plan. Much of *Walker's Appeal* is addressed particularly to slaves, urging them to rise up and take the freedom due them, by any means possible.

'Never make an attempt to gain our freedom or natural right, from under our cruel oppressors and murderers, until you see your way clear—when that hour arrives and you move, be not afraid or dismayed . . .

. . . if you commence kill or be killed. Now, I ask you, had you not rather be killed than to be a slave to a tyrant, who takes the life of your mother, wife and dear little children?. . . believe this, that it is no more harm for you to kill a man, who is trying to kill you, than it is for you to take a drink of water when thirsty . . .'

Walker also addressed part of his message to white Americans:

'If any are anxious to ascertain who I am, know the world, that I am one of the oppressed, degraded and wretched sons of Africa, rendered so by the avaricious and unmerciful, among the whites. If any wish to plunge me into the wretched incapacity of a slave, or murder me for the truth, know ye, that I am in the hand of God, and at your disposal. I count my life not dear unto me, but I am ready to be offered at any moment. For what is the use of living, when in fact I am dead. But remember, Americans, that as miserable, wretched, degraded and abject as you have made us in preceding, and in this generation, to support you and your families, that some of you (whites) on the continent of America, will yet curse the day that you ever were born. You want slaves, and want us for your slaves!!! My colour will yet, root some of you out of the very face of the earth!!!!!!'

William Lloyd Garrison's Liberator

William Lloyd Garrison

On January 1, 1831, William Lloyd Garrison (1805–1879) began publishing his anti-slavery newspaper, The Liberator. *Many historians date the beginning of the Abolitionist movement and Northern interest in the Underground Railway from the appearance of this publication.*

A white Bostonian, Garrison condemned slavery as a national sin, called for immediate emancipation, and suggested ways of integrating the freed slaves into society. Garrison referred to David Walker's Appeal *as "one of the most remarkable productions of the age" and the "forerunner of the Abolition struggle." Just a few years after Walker, Garrison published his own "Manifesto."*

Source: William Lloyd Garrison, "Manifesto," *The Liberator*, Jan. 1, 1831.

In defending the great cause of human rights, I wish to derive the assistance of all religions and of all parties.

Assenting to the "self-evident truth" maintained in the American Declaration of Independence, "that all men are created equal, and endowed by their creator with certain inalienable rights—among which are life, liberty and the pursuit of happiness," I shall strenuously contend for the immediate enfranchisement of our slave population. . . .

I am aware, that many object to the severity of my language; but is there not cause for severity? I *will be* as harsh as truth, and as uncompromising as justice. On this subject, I do not wish to think, or speak, or write, with moderation. No! no! Tell a man whose house is on fire, to give a moderate alarm; tell him to moderately rescue his wife from the hands of the ravisher; tell the mother to gradually extricate her babe from the fire into which it has fallen; —but urge me not to use moderation in a cause like the present. I am in earnest—I will not equivocate—I will not excuse—I will not retreat a single inch—AND I WILL BE HEARD.

William Lloyd Garrison
Boston, January 1, 1831

The Fugitive Slave Acts

Responding to pressure from the Southern states, Congress passed laws in 1793 and in 1850 that provided for the capture and return of runaway slaves who had escaped from one state to another. The 1793 law authorized judges and state magistrates to decide the status of an alleged runaway slave without the benefit of a jury trial. In opposition, some Northern states enacted personal-liberty laws providing that fugitives who appealed such decisions against them were entitled to a jury trial. Many individuals who opposed the law of 1793 became active in helping slaves escape by the Underground Railroad.

The Southern states demanded more effective legislation, and a second Fugitive Slave Act was passed in 1850. Under this law, fugitives were not only forbidden trial by jury but also were prevented from testifying on their own behalf. Heavy penalties were provided for federal marshals who refused to enforce the laws and on any individuals who helped slaves escape. Special commissioners were appointed to enforce the law. The measure was so severe that it actually defeated its purpose—anti-slavery activity increased, and the Underground Railroad became more efficient. Many Northern states enacted new personal-liberty laws to counter the slave act, which was finally repealed in 1864.

The text of the Fugitive Slave Act of 1850 follows.

Source: Fugitive Slave Act, Thirty-first Congress, Sess. I Ch. 60 (1850).

Be it enacted by the Senate and House of Representatives of the United States of America in congress assembled,

. . . That when a person held to service or labor in any State or Territory of the United States, has heretofore or shall here-after escape into another State or Territory of the United States, the person or persons to whom such service or labor may be due, or his, her, or their agent or attorney, . . . may pursue and reclaim such fugitive person, either by procuring a warrant . . . or by seizing and arresting such fugitive, where the same can be done without process, and by taking, or causing such person to be taken, forthwith before such court, judge, or commissioner, whose duty it shall be to hear and determine the case of such claimant in a summary manner; and upon satisfactory proof being made, by deposition or affidavit, . . . or by other satisfactory testimony, duly taken and certified . . . to make out and deliver to such claimant, his or her agent or attorney, a certificate setting forth the substantial facts as to the service or labor due from such fugitive to the claimant, and of his or her escape from the State or Territory in which such service or labor was due, to the State or Territory in which he or she was arrested, with authority to such claimant, or his or her agent or attorney, to use such reasonable force and restraint as may be necessary, under the circumstances of the case, to take and remove such fugitive person back to the State or Territory whence he or she may have escaped as aforesaid. *In no trial or hearing under this act shall the testimony of such alleged fugitive be admitted in evidence;* [emphasis added] and the certificates . . . shall be conclusive of the right of the person or persons in whose favor granted, to remove such fugitive to the State or Territory from which he escaped, and shall prevent all molesta-

CAUTION!!

COLORED PEOPLE

OF BOSTON, ONE & ALL,

You are hereby respectfully **CAUTIONED** and advised, to avoid conversing with the

Watchmen and Police Officers of Boston,

For since the recent **ORDER OF THE MAYOR & ALDERMEN,** they are empowered to act as

KIDNAPPERS

AND

Slave Catchers,

And they have already been actually employed in **KIDNAPPING, CATCHING, AND KEEPING SLAVES.** Therefore, if you value your **LIBERTY,** and the *Welfare of the Fugitives* among you, *Shun* them in every possible manner, as so many *HOUNDS* on the track of the most unfortunate of your race.

Keep a Sharp Look Out for KIDNAPPERS, and have TOP EYE open.

APRIL 24, 1851.

tion of such person or persons by any process issued by any court, judge, magistrate, or other person whomsoever.

And be it further enacted, That any person who shall knowingly and willingly obstruct, hinder, or prevent such claimant, his agent or attorney, or any person or persons lawfully assisting him, her, or them, from arresting such a fugitive from service or labor, either with or without process as aforesaid, or shall rescue, or attempt to rescue, such fugitive from service or labor, from the custody of such claimant, his or her agent or attorney, or other person or persons lawfully assisting as aforesaid, when so arrested, pursuant to the authority herein given and declared; or shall aid, abet, or assist such person so owing service or labor—as aforesaid, directly or indirectly, to escape from such claimant, his agent or attorney, or other person or persons legally authorized as aforesaid; or shall harbor or conceal such fugitive, so as to prevent the discovery and arrest of such person, after notice or knowledge of the fact that such person was a fugitive, from service or labor as aforesaid, shall, for either of said offences, be subject to a fine not exceeding one thousand dollars, and imprisonment not exceeding six months, by indictment and conviction before the District Court of the United States for the district in which such offence may have been committed, or before the proper court of criminal jurisdiction, if committed within any one of the organized Territories of the United States; and shall moreover forfeit and pay, by way of civil damages to the party injured by such illegal conduct, the sum of one thousand dollars, for each fugitive so lost as aforesaid, to be recovered by action of debt, in any of the District or Territorial Courts aforesaid, within whose jurisdiction the said offence may have been committed. . . .

APPROVED, September 18, 1850.

24

Harriet Beecher Stowe's Uncle Tom's Cabin

Harriet Beecher Stowe (1811-1896) was a minister's daughter and became a minister's wife. She taught school in Connecticut and in Ohio, where she began to write stories and essays. In Cincinnati, she came in contact with the Underground Railroad. From fugitives and friends, Stowe learned about life in the Southern states, which she later visited. In 1850 the family moved to Maine, where Stowe wrote Uncle Tom's Cabin; or, Life Among the Lowly. *The novel about the horrors of slavery was first published as a serial in the* National Era, *an antislavery paper of Washington, D.C.*

Uncle Tom's Cabin *became incredibly popular and influential (except in the South) and is sometimes counted among the causes of the Civil War. It was translated into at least 23 languages, and a theatrical adaptation played to capacity audiences. Stowe was influenced by slave narratives, including the writings of Frederick Douglass and Lewis Clarke. In 1854, she published* The Key to Uncle Tom's Cabin, *a collection of documents and testimonies against slavery.*

*Poster advertising the
sale of* Uncle Tom's Cabin.

Signs and Songs to Follow

Once a slave decided to escape, how was he or she to know how and where to go? In the Southern states, escapees were generally on their own; if the fugitives succeeded in moving North, they could find more help.

Former slaves who had escaped passed useful information back to those still in bondage. Fugitives learned to follow the North Star, and found that tree moss (which grew on the north side of trees) could give them a clue to directions on cloudy nights

Underground Railroad operators put out signals—a strategically placed lantern or candle, or a particular kind of quilt hanging on a laundry line. Quilts with star patterns were said to point out the right direction, while a design of a house with smoke coming from the chimney indicated a friendly stopping place. Some quilts were said to encode information about way stations. When the signs indicated a safe haven, the refugees might find food and rest in hidden rooms, attics, and cellars. Otherwise, they had to return to the hills, swamps, caves, and forests to hide.

Some historians believe that the Log Cabin quilt design shown here was a sign of a safe house when it had a black center. The pattern most often had a red center.

Spirituals

Sometimes codes were hidden in popular songs and spirituals. For example, although some songs mentioned Canada openly, others disguised it as Canaan.

Source: Charles L. Blockson in *National Geographic*, 1984. Found on "The Underground Railroad Site." http://education.ucdavis.edu/NEW/STC/lesson/socstud/railroad/music.htm.

Frederick Douglass wrote that "A keen observer may have detected Canada in our repeated singings of:

> 'O Canaan, sweet Canaan,
> I am bound for the land of Canaan.'

Lines such as "Comin' for to carry me home" in the spiritual "Swing Low, Sweet Chariot" might well refer to the arrival of an Underground Railroad conductor.

Swing Low, Sweet Chariot

Chorus
Swing low, sweet chariot,
Comin' for to carry me home,
Swing low, sweet chariot,
Comin' for to carry me home.

I look'd over Jordan an' what did I see,
Comin' for to carry me home,
A band of angels comin' after me,
Comin' for to carry me home.

If you get there before I do,
Comin' for to carry me home,
Tell all my friends I'm comin' there too,
Comin' for to carry me home.

Chorus

One popular song referred to the Big Dipper and North star by which refugees navigated. A carpenter called Peg Leg Joe used to travel from farm to farm, teaching slaves the song "Follow the Drinking Gourd," to remind them how to find their way North.

Source: The song and notes that follow were found on "Follow the Drinking Gourd," the Oklahoma Baptist University Planetarium website: http://www.okbu.edu/academics/natsci/planet/shows/gourd.htm.

Follow the Drinking Gourd

When the Sun comes back
And the first quail calls[1]
Follow the Drinking Gourd.
For the old man[2] is a-waiting for to carry you to freedom
If you follow the Drinking Gourd.

The riverbank[3] makes a very good road.
The dead trees will show you the way.
Left foot, peg foot, traveling on,[4]
Follow the Drinking Gourd.

The river ends between two hills
Follow the Drinking Gourd.
There's another river on the other side[5]
Follow the Drinking Gourd.

When the great big river meets the little river[6]
Follow the Drinking Gourd.
For the old man is a-waiting for to carry you to freedom
If you follow the drinking gourd.

---

[1] On the winter solstice the Sun rises in the southeast. In the months after the December solstice the Sun rises more northerly and ascends higher in the sky each day. Migratory quail winter in the south.

[2] Peg Leg Joe.

[3] Tombiggee River, leading northward from the Gulf of Mexico toward Tennessee.

[4] Dead trees were used as markers with charcoal and mud drawings of a peg leg and a foot.

[5] Tennessee River, which flows northward across Tennessee and Kentucky.

[6] At the confluence of the Tennessee River and the Ohio River (over 800 miles north of Mobile), where Underground Railroad guides would meet fugitive slaves on the northern bank and transport them to safer regions. A slave who left a farm or plantation in southern Alabama or Mississippi in the winter (see note 1) would arrive at the Ohio river about a year later—the best time to cross, when one could simply walk across the ice.

Other spirituals were openly about escape, and an invitation for others to escape, such as this "Song of the Fugitive."

Source: George M. Allen, "Rare Song Collection", University of Michigan. Found in Dr. Bryan E. Walls, *The Road That Led to Somewhere*. Ontario, Canada: Olive Publishing Company Ltd. 1980, pp. 103-104.

Song of the Fugitive

I'm on my way to Canada a freeman's rights to share;
The cruel wrongs of slavery I can no longer bear;
My heart is crushed within me, so while I remain a slave
I am resolved to strike the blow for freedom or the grave.

O Great Father, do thou pity me,
And help me on to Canada
Where panting slave is free.

I've served my Master all my days without the least reward;
And now I'm forced to flee away to shun the lash abhorred.
The hounds are baying on my tracks; my Master's just behind,
Resolved that he will bring me back and fast his fetters bind.

I heard that Queen Victoria has pledged us all a home
Beyond the reach of slavery, if we will only come,
So I have fled this weary way, my guide the bright North Star.
And now, thank God, I speed the day in the underground railcar,

O, Old Master, why come after me?
I'm whizzing fast to Canada
Where the panting slave is freed.

I now embark for yonder shore, sweet land of liberty;
Our vessel soon will bear me o'er, and I shall then be free,
No more I'll dread the auctioneer, nor fear the Master's frowns;
No more I'll tremble lest I hear the baying of the hounds.

O, Old Master, 'tis vain to follow me;
I'm just in sight of Canada
Where the panting slave is free.

Yes! I am safe in Canada—my soul and body free,
My blood and tears no more shall drench thy soil, O Carolina,
Yet how can I suppress the tear that's starting from my eyes
To think my friends and kindred dear as slaves must live and die.

O dear friends, haste and follow me.
For I am safe in Canada
Where the panting slave is free.

Going in Disguise

Whether they traveled on their own or made use of the Underground Railroad, fugitives often disguised themselves cleverly. For example, women sometimes dressed as men, and men dressed as women. Some faked messages or goods to deliver for their masters. Light-skinned African Americans could pass as white, perhaps as the master of a darker-skinned companion.

Anna Maria Weems as a Male

Fifteen-year-old Anna Weems used several male aliases to escape bondage. Anna's family members had all been sold before she was thirteen, and she became determined not to spend her life as a slave. After taking the Underground Railroad to New York, Weems moved on to Canada where she got an education.

Source: William Still, "The Underground Railroad," 1870. Found on The Underground Railroad Site: http://education.ucdavis.edu/NEW/STC/lesson/socstud/railroad.htm.

The only chance of procuring her freedom, depended upon getting her away on the Underground Rail Road. She was neatly attired in male habiliments, and in that manner came all the way from Washington. After passing two or three days with her new friends in Philadelphia, she was sent on (in male attire) to Lewis Tappan, of New York, who had likewise been deeply interested in her case from the beginning, and who held himself ready, as was understood, to cash a draft for three hundred dollars to compensate the man who might risk his own liberty in bringing her on from Washington. After having arrived safely in New York, she found a home and kind friends in the family of Rev. A. N. Freeman, and received quite an ovation characteristic of an Underground Rail Road.

William and Ellen Craft as Master and Slave

The Crafts were a married slave couple who thought up a clever way to escape together.

Source: William Still, The *Underground Rail Road - A Record of Facts, Authentic Narratives, Letters.* (Originally published in 1871) Chicago: Johnson Publishing Company Inc., 1970, pp. 382-384.

A quarter of a century ago, William and Ellen Craft were slaves in the State of Georgia. With them, as with thousands of others, the desire to be free was very strong. For this jewel they were willing to make any sacrifice, or to endure any amount of suffering. In this state of mind they commenced planning. After thinking of various ways that might be tried, it occurred to William and Ellen, that one might act the part of master and the other the part of servant.

Ellen being fair enough to pass for white, of necessity would have to be transformed into a young planter for the time being. All that was needed, however, to make this important change was that she should be dressed elegantly in a fashionable suit of male attire, and have her hair cut in the style usually worn by young planters. Her profusion of dark hair offered a fine opportunity for the change. So far this plan looked very tempting. But it occurred to them that Ellen was beardless. After some mature reflection, they came to the conclusion that this difficulty could be very readily obviated by having the face muffled up as though the young planter was suffering badly with the face or toothache; thus they got rid of this trouble. Straightway, upon further reflection, several other very serious difficulties stared them in the face. For instance, in traveling, they knew that they would be under the necessity of stopping repeatedly at hotels, and that the custom of registering would have to be conformed to, un-less some very good excuse could be given for not doing so.

Here they again thought much over matters, and wisely concluded that the young man had better assume the attitude of a gentleman very much indisposed. He must have his right arm placed carefully in a sling; that would be a sufficient excuse for not registering, etc. Then he must be a little lame, with a nice cane in the left hand; he must have large green spectacles over his eyes, and withal he must be very hard of hearing and dependent on his faithful servant (as was no uncommon thing with slave-holders), to look after all his wants.

Ellen, in disguise

William was just the man to act this part. To begin with, he was very "likely-looking;" smart, active and exceedingly attentive to his young master—indeed he was almost eyes, ears, hands and feet for him. William knew that this would please the slave-holders. The young planter would have nothing to do but hold himself subject to his ailments and put on a bold air of superiority; he was not to deign to notice anybody. If, while traveling, gentlemen, either politely or rudely, should venture to scrape acquaintance with the young planter, in his deafness he was to remain mute; the servant was to explain. In every instance when this occurred, as it actually did, the servant was fully equal to the emergency—none dreamed of the disguises in which the Underground Rail Road passengers were traveling.

They stopped at a first-class hotel in Charleston, where the young planter and his body servant were treated, as the house was wont to treat the chivalry. They stopped also at a similar hotel in Richmond, and with like results.

They knew that they must pass through Baltimore, but they did not know the obstacles that they would have to surmount in the Monumental City. They proceeded to the depot in the usual manner, and the servant asked for tickets for his master and self. Of course the master could have a ticket, but "bonds will have to be entered before you can get a ticket," said the ticket master. "It is the rule of this office to require bonds for all negroes applying for tickets to go North, and none but gentlemen of well-known responsibility will be taken," further explained the ticket master.

The servant replied, that he knew "nothing about that" —that he was "simply traveling with his young master to take care of him—he being in a very delicate state of health, so much so, that fears were entertained that he might not be able to hold out to reach Philadelphia, where he was hastening for medical treatment," and ended his reply by saying, "my master can't be detained." Without further parley, the ticket master very obligingly waived the old "rule," and furnished the requisite tickets. The mountain being thus removed, the young planter and his faithful servant were safely in the cars for the city of Brotherly Love.

Scarcely had they arrived on free soil when the rheumatism departed—the right arm was unslung—the toothache was gone—the beardless face was unmuffled—the deaf heard and spoke—the blind saw and the lame leaped as an hart, and in the presence of a few astonished friends of the slave, the facts of this unparalleled Underground Rail Road feat were fully established by the most unquestionable evidence.

Frederick Douglass as a Sailor

In his 1845 autobiography, Frederick Douglass warned against giving away too much information about escape routes. Some published narratives, he said, "do nothing towards enlightening the slave, whilst they do much towards enlightening the master. They stimulate him to greater watchfulness, and enhance his power to capture his slave. . . . we should be careful to do nothing which would be likely to hinder the former from escaping from slavery. I would keep the merciless slaveholder profoundly ignorant of the means of flight adopted by the slave." (Source: Frederick Douglass, Narrative of the Life of Frederick Douglass, An American Slave, Written by Himself. *Boston: 1845; New York: Doubleday & Co., 1963, p. 100.)*

Forty years later, when the information could do no harm, Douglass finally published the story of his escape.

Source: Douglass, Frederick. "My Escape from Slavery," *The Century Illustrated Magazine 23*, n.s. 1 (Nov. 1881), pp. 125-131. Found on "History—the 19th Century," Site: http://history1800s.about.com/msubslavery.htm.

It was the custom in the State of Maryland to require the free colored people to have what were called free papers. These instruments they were required to renew very often, and by charging a fee for this writing, considerable sums from time to time were collected by the State. In these papers the name, age, color, height, and form of the freeman were described, together with any scars or other marks upon his person which could assist in his identification. This device in some measure defeated itself—since more than one man could be found to answer the same general description. Hence many slaves could escape by personating the owner of one set of papers; and this was often done as follows: A slave, nearly or sufficiently answering the description set forth in the papers, would borrow or hire them till by means of them he could escape to a free State, and then, by mail or otherwise, would return them to the owner. The operation was a hazardous one for the lender as well as for the borrower. A failure on the part of the fugitive to send back the papers would imperil his benefactor, and the discovery of the papers in possession of the wrong man would imperil both the fugitive and his friend. It was, therefore, an act of supreme trust on the part of a freeman of color thus to put in jeopardy his own liberty that another might be free. It was, however, not unfrequently bravely done, and was seldom discovered. I was not so fortunate as to resemble any of my free acquaintances sufficiently to answer the description of their papers. But I had a friend—a sailor —who owned a sailor's protection, which answered somewhat the purpose of free papers—describing his person, and certifying to the fact that he was a free American sailor. The instrument had at its head the American eagle, which gave it the appearance at once of an authorized document. This protection, when in my hands, did not describe its bearer very accurately. Indeed, it called for a man much darker than myself, and close examination of it would have caused my arrest at the start.

In order to avoid this fatal scrutiny on the part of railroad officials, I arranged with Isaac Rolls, a Baltimore hackman, to bring my baggage to the Philadelphia train just on the moment of starting, and jumped upon the car myself when the train was in motion. Had I gone into the station and offered to purchase a ticket, I should have been instantly and carefully examined, and undoubtedly arrested. In choosing this plan I considered the jostle of the train, and the natural haste of the conductor, in a train crowded with passengers, and relied upon my skill and address in playing the sailor, as described in my protection, to do the rest. One element in my favor was the kind feeling which prevailed in Baltimore and other sea-ports at the time, toward "those who go down to the sea in ships." "Free trade and sailors' rights" just then expressed the sentiment of the country. In my clothing I was rigged out in sailor style. I had on a red shirt and a tarpaulin hat, and a black cravat tied in sailor fashion carelessly and loosely about my neck. My knowledge of ships and sailor's talk came much to my assistance, for I knew a ship from stem to stern, and from keelson to cross-trees, and could talk sailor like an "old salt." I was well on the way to Havre de Grace before the conductor came into the negro car to collect tickets and examine the papers of his black passengers. This was a critical moment in the drama. My whole future depended upon the decision of this conductor. Agitated though I was while this ceremony was proceeding, still, externally, at least, I was apparently calm and self-possessed. He went on with his duty—examining several colored passengers before reaching me. He was somewhat harsh in tone and peremptory in manner until he reached me, when, strange enough, and to my surprise and relief, his whole manner changed. Seeing that I did not readily produce my free papers, as the other colored persons in the car had done, he said to me, in friendly contrast with his bearing toward the others:

"I suppose you have your free papers?"

To which I answered: "No sir; I never carry my free papers to sea with me."

"But you have something to show that you are a freeman, haven't you?"

"Yes, sir," I answered; "I have a paper with the American Eagle on it, and that will carry me around the world."

With this I drew from my deep sailor's pocket my seaman's protection, as before described. The merest glance at the paper satisfied him, and he took my fare and went on about his business. This moment of time was one of the most anxious I ever experienced. Had the conductor looked closely at the paper, he could not have failed to discover that it called for a very different-looking person from my-self, and in that case it would have been his duty to arrest me on the instant, and send me back to Baltimore from the first station. When he left me with the assurance that I was all right, though much relieved, I realized that I was still in great danger: I was still in Maryland, and subject to arrest at any moment. I saw on the train several persons who would have known me in any other clothes, and I feared they might recognize me, even in my sailor "rig," and report me to the conductor, who would then subject me to a closer examina-tion, which I knew well would be fatal to me. Though I was not a murderer fleeing from justice, I felt perhaps quite as miserable as such a criminal. The train was moving at a very high rate of speed for that epoch of railroad travel, but to my anxious mind it was moving far too slowly. Minutes were hours, and hours were days during this part of my flight. After Maryland, I was to pass through Delaware—another slave State, where slave-catchers generally awaited their prey, for it was not in the interior of the State, but on its borders, that these human hounds were most vigilant and active. The border lines between slavery and freedom were the dangerous ones for the fugitives. The heart of no fox or deer, with hungry hounds on his trail in full chase, could have beaten more anxiously or noisily than did mine from the time I left Baltimore till I reached Philadelphia. The passage of the Susquehanna River at Havre de Grace was at that time made by ferry-boat, on board of which I met a young colored man by the name of Nichols, who came very near betraying me. He was a "hand" on the boat, but, instead of minding his business, he insisted upon knowing me, and asking me dangerous questions as to where I was going, when I was coming back, etc. I got away from my old and inconvenient acquaintance as soon as I could decently do so, and went to another part of the boat. Once across the river, I encountered a new danger. Only a few days before, I had been at work on a revenue cutter, in Mr. Price's ship-yard in Baltimore, under the care of Captain McGowan. On the meeting at this point of the two trains, the one going south stopped on the track just opposite to the one going north, and it so happened that this Captain McGowan sat at a window where he could see me very distinctly, and would certainly have recognized me had he looked at me but for a second. Fortunately, in the hurry of the moment, he did not see me; and the trains soon passed each other on their respective ways. But this was not my only hair-breadth escape. A German blacksmith whom I knew well was on the train with me, and looked at me very intently, as if he thought he had seen me somewhere before in his travels. I really believe he knew me, but had no heart to betray me. At any rate, he saw me escaping and held his peace.

The last point of imminent danger, and the one I dreaded most, was Wilmington. Here we left the train and took the steam-boat for Philadelphia. In making the change here I again apprehended arrest, but no one disturbed me, and I was soon on the broad and beautiful Delaware, speeding away to the Quaker City. On reaching Philadelphia in the afternoon, I inquired of a colored man how I could get on to New York. He directed me to the William-street depot, and thither I went, taking the train that night. I reached New York Tuesday morning, having completed the journey in less than twenty-four hours.

Henry Brown as a Package

Perhaps the most unusual—and uncomfortable—disguise was that of Henry "Box" Brown, who shipped himself by train in a wooden crate. Unfortunately, the baggage handlers paid little attention to the sign that indicated "this side up with care."

Source: George Steams, *Narrative of Henry Box Brown by Himself*, Boston, 1849, pp. 60-62.

I took my place in this narrow prison, with a mind full of uncertainty as to the result. It was a critical period of my life, I can assure you, reader; but if you have never been deprived of your liberty, as I was, you cannot realize the power of that hope of freedom. . . .

I laid me down in my darkened home of three feet by two, and . . . resigned myself to my fate. My friend was to accompany me but he failed to do so; and contented himself with sending a telegraph message to his correspondent in Philadelphia, that such a box was on its way to his care.

I took with me a bladder filled with water to bathe my neck with, in case of too great heat; and with no access to the fresh air, excepting three small . . . holes, I started on my perilous cruise. I was first carried to the express office, the box being placed on its end, so that I started with my head downwards, although the box was directed, "this side up with care." From the express office, I was carried to the depot, and from thence tumbled roughly into the baggage car, where I happened to fall "right side up," but no thanks to my transporters. But after a while the cars stopped, and I was put aboard a steamboat, and placed on my head. In this dreadful position, I remained the space of an hour and a half, it seemed to me when I began to feel of my eyes and head, and found to my dismay, that my eyes were almost swollen out of their sockets, and the veins on my temple seemed ready to burst. I made no noise however, determining to obtain "victory or death," but endured the terrible pain, as well as I could, sustained under the whole by the thoughts of sweet liberty. About half an hour afterwards, I attempted again to lift my hands to my face, but I found I was not able to move them. A cold sweat now covered me from head to foot. . . . One-half hour longer and my sufferings would have ended in that fate, which I preferred to slavery; but I lifted up my heart to God in prayer, believing that he would yet deliver me, when to my joy, I overheard two men say, "We have been here two hours and have travelled twenty miles, now let us sit down, and rest ourselves." They turned the box over, containing my soul and body, thus delivering me from the power of the grim messenger of death, who a few moments previously had aimed his fatal shaft at my head, and had placed his icy hands on my throbbing heart. One of these men inquired of the other, what he supposed that box contained, to which his comrade replied, that he guessed it was the mail. "Yes," I thought, "it is a male, indeed, although not the mail of the United States."

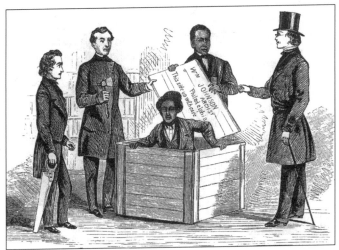

Resurrection of Henry "Box" Brown.

Soon after this fortunate event, we arrived at Washington, where I was thrown from the wagon, and again as my luck would have it, fell on my head. . . . Pretty soon, I heard some one say, "there is no room for this box, it will have to remain behind." I then again applied to the Lord, my help in all my difficulties, and in a few minutes I heard a gentleman direct the hands to place it aboard, as "it came with the mail and must go on with it." I was then tumbled into the car, my head downwards again, as I seemed to be destined to escape on my head. . . . We had not proceeded far, however, before more baggage was placed in the car, at a stopping place, and I was again turned to my proper position. No farther difficulty occurred until my arrival in Philadelphia. I reached this place at three o'clock in the morning, and remained in the depot until six o'clock A.M., at which time, a wagon drove up. . . . I was soon placed on this wagon, and carried to the house of my friend's correspondent, where quite a number of persons were waiting to receive me. There 17 appeared to be some afraid to open the box at first, but at length one of them rapped upon it, and with a trembling voice, asked, "Is all right within?" to which I replied, "All right." The joy of these friends was excessive . . . each one seized hold of some tool, and commenced opening my grave. At length the cover was removed, and I arose, and shook myself . . . and I swooned away.

Stories of the Long Hard Trip

Many stories of the Underground Railroad were recorded in narratives, written or dictated by those who escaped. In 1760, A Narrative of the Uncommon Sufferings and Surprising Deliverance of Briton Hammon, a Negro Man, *was published in Boston. It was soon to be followed by others, and in the nineteenth century the Abolitionists actively encouraged such accounts. Many fugitive narratives, such as* Scenes in the Life of Harriet Tubman *(1869), are accurate autobiographies, though others were expanded and fictionalized. Perhaps the most famous is* Narrative of the Life of Frederick Douglass, an American Slave; Written by Himself *(1845).*

In the mid-nineteenth century, the Reverend Nehemiah Adams of Boston published A South-Side View of Slavery, *suggesting that slave owners were "the guardians, educators, and saviors of the African race in this country." About that time, 2000 federal troops were called out in Boston to aid in the capture and conviction of runaway slave Anthony Burns. In response to these and other events, Boston educator and journalist Benjamin Drew decided to publish the fugitive's point of view. He went to Canada to hear the stories of former slaves firsthand. By that time, the fugitives in Canada numbered about 30,000. Drew interviewed scores of them and wrote down their words, changing their names to protect their identities.*

In 1855 Drew published his collection of fugitive narratives as A North-Side View of Slavery. *Other similar collections were published in the nineteenth century, and today the slave narratives are recognized as an American literary genre.*

Help along the Way

Seventeen-year-old James Adams was accompanied by his cousin, Benjamin Harris on his flight to freedom. Along the way, the two had to decide who they could trust—and when to run.

Source James Adams, Benjamin Drew, ed., *The Refugee: or Narratives of Fugitive Slaves in Canada Related by Themselves.* Boston, 1856.

. . . .We started away at night, on the 12th of August 1824. After we had crossed the river, alarm was given, and my father came down where we had crossed, and called to me to come back. I had not told my intention to either my father or mother. I made no answer at all, but we walked three miles back from the river, where we lay concealed in the woods four days. The nights we passed at the house of a white friend; a friend indeed. We set out on a Monday night, and on the night following, seven more of my fellow-servants started on the same race. They were overtaken on Wednesday night, while they were in a house on the Ohio side. One jumped from a window and broke his arm; he stayed in the woods some days, and then he returned. The other six, two women and four children, were carried back, and the man we stopped with told us that the two women were whipped to make them tell where we were, so they could come upon us. They told their master as near as they could. On Thursday five white men came to the house where we had been concealed, but we were then in the woods and mountains, three miles from the friend's house. Every evening, between three and four o'clock, he would come and bring us food. We had nothing to give him—it was the hand of Divine Providence made him do it. He and others on the river see so much abuse of colored people that they pity them, and so are ready to give them aid; at least it was so then. He told the white men he knew nothing about us, and nothing of the kind. They searched his premises, and then left, believing his story. He came to us and said, "Boys, we are betrayed, they are coming now round the hill after us." We picked up our bundles and started on a run; then he called us back, and said he did it to try our *spunk*. He then told us of those who were carried back, and of the searching of his premises. We lodged in his barn that night . . .

[Later in our escape, a friend] pointed out a haystack, where we were to rendezvous at night, to meet another man whom our friend was to send to take us further along on our way. At night we went to the haystack; a road ran by it. Instead of keeping watch by the stack, we were so jaded that we crossed the road and lay down to rest on the bare ground, where we fell asleep. The man, as we afterwards learned from him, came as agreed upon, whistled and made signals, but failed to wake us up. Thinking we had been pursued away, he went back without us. The next morning, when we awoke, the sun was rising red, right on the public road. We saw a man at his door some two hundred yards from us. I went to ask him how the roads ran; [Ben] told me to inquire the way to Carr's Run, near home, so we would go the contrary. By the time I got back, Ben, who had watched, saw the man leave his house with his gun, and take a circle round to come down on us; but before he could head us, we were past him in the road running. We ran and walked about four miles barefoot; then we took courage to put on our shoes, which we had not dared stop long enough to do before, . . .

Presently we came to a toll-gate, about which there were standing several white men. We walked up boldly to the gate; one of the men then asked us, "Where are you going?" Ben answered, "We are going to Chillicothe to see our friends there." Then he made answer and said, "You can't go any further, you must go back with me, you are the very boys I was looking for last night." We told him we wanted to go on, but he said, "There are so many buckskin Yankees in these parts that you will be taken before you get half through the town. We then went back to his house, but we did not stop more than ten minutes, because it would be dangerous for him as well as for us if we were caught on his premises. He stuck up a pole close to his house and tied a white cloth on it; then he led us up to the top of the hill (this was Monday, quite early in the morning), and showed us a rough ace of bushes and rocks where we could lie concealed quite pleasantly, and so high up that we could see the main road, and the toll-gate, and the house, and the white flag. Said he, "If there's any danger, I'll send a child out to throw down the white flag; and if you get scared away from here, come back at night and I'll protect you." Soon after he left us, we saw five white men come to his house on horseback; they were the five who had carried back the others that tried to escape. Two of them went into the house; then we saw a little girl come out and climb up on the fence, as if she were playing about, and she knocked down the flagpole—which meant that we were to look out for ourselves. But we did not feel that there was any immediate danger, and so we kept close under cover. Pretty soon the two came out of the house, and they all rode forward very fast, passed the toll-gate, and were soon out of sight. I suppose they thought to overtake us every minute, but luckily I have never seen them since. In the evening the man came and conducted us to his house, where we found the men we had seen at the toll-gate in the morning. They were mostly armed with pistols and guns. They guided us to a solitary house three miles back among the mountains, in the neighborhood of which we remained three days. We were told to go up on the mountain very high, where was an Indian cave in the rocks. From this cave we could look a great distance around and see people, and we felt afraid they would see us. So instead of staying there, we went down the mountain to a creek where trees had been cut down and branches thrown over the bank; we went under the branches and bushes where the sand was dry, and there we would sit all day. We all the time talked to each other about how we would get away, and what we should do if the white folks tackled us; that was all our discourse.

We stayed there until Friday, when our friends gave us knapsacks full of cakes and dried venison, and a little bundle of provision besides, and flints and steel, and spunk, and a pocket-compass to travel through the woods by.

....

Our feet were now sore with long travelling. One night we came to a river; it was rather foggy, but I could see a ferry-scow on the other side. I was afraid of alligators, but I swam over, and poled the scow back and ferried Ben across,—his ankle was so sore, that he did not like to put his foot in the water if he could help it. We soon reached an old stable in the edge of a little town; we entered it and slept alternately one keeping watch, as we always managed while in the neighborhood of settlements. We did not do this in the wilderness,—*there* we slept safely, and were quite *reconciled*. At cock-crowing in the morning we set out and went into the woods, which were very near; there we stayed through the day.

At night we started on and presently came into a road running north-west. Coming to a vine patch we filled our knapsacks with cucumbers; we then met a white man, who asked us, "Which way are you travelling?" My cousin told him "To Cleveland, to help a man drive a drove of cattle." He then said, "I know you must be runaways,—but you needn't be afraid of me,—I don't want to hurt you." He then told us something that we knew before—that the last spring five fugitives were overtaken at his house by my master and two other men; that the fugitives took through his wheat-field,—one of them, a little fellow, could not run so fast as the rest, and master called to him to stop, or he'd shoot him. His answer was, "shoot and be d—d!" The man further told us, that he took through the wheat-field as if he would assist in catching the slaves, but that when he got near enough, he told them to "push on!" Ben and I knew about the pursuit, and what the little fellow had said; for it got round among the servants, after master got back. That little fellow's widow is now my wife. We went to the man's house, and partook of a good luncheon. He told us to hurry, and try to get through Newark [Ohio] before daylight. We hurried accordingly, but it was daybreak when we crossed the bridge. We found the little toll-gate open and we went through—there were lights in a tavern window at the left of the gate, and the windows had no curtains. Just as we were stepping off the bridge, a plank rattled,—then up started after us a little black dog, making a great noise. We walked smartly along, but did not run until we came to a street leading to the right,—then we ran fast until we came to a left hand turn, which led to the main road at the other side of the town. Before sunrise, we hid in a thicket of briars, close by the road, where we lay all day, seeing the teams, and every thing that passed by.

At dark we went on again, passed through Mount Vernon [Ohio] in the night, and kept on until daylight. Again we halted in concealment until night, then we went on again through Wooster. After leaving Wooster, we saw no more settlements, except one little village, which we passed through in broad day. We entered a store here, but were asked no questions. Here we learned the way to Cleveland. In the middle of the afternoon we stopped for a little rest. Just before night we moved forward again and travelled all night. We then stopped to rest until four in the afternoon, mean-while roasting some corn as before. At about four, we met a preacher, who was just come from Cleveland. He asked us if we were making our escape,—we told him "No." He said, "You need not be afraid of me,—I am the friend of all who travel from the South to the North." He told us not to go into Cleveland, as we would be taken up. He then described a house which was on our way, where, he said, we might mention our meeting him, and we would find friends who would put us on board a boat. We hid until dark,—then we went to the house, which we recognized readily from the preacher's description. We knocked at the door, and were invited in. My cousin told them what the minister had said. The man of the house hid us in his barn two nights and three days. He was a shoemaker. The next night after we got there, he went to Cleveland himself to get a berth for us aboard some boat for Canada. When he returned, he said he had found a passage for us with Capt. B., who was to sail the next Thursday at 10 P.M. At that hour we embarked, having a free passage in a schooner for Buffalo. On board this boat, we met with an Englishman whom we had often seen on a steamboat at the plantation. He knew us, and told us a reward of one hundred dollars was offered for each of us, and he showed us several handbills to that effect. He said they had been given him to put up along the road, but he had preferred to keep them in his pocket. Capt. B. took away our knives and Ben's tomahawk, for fear of mischief.

We reached Buffalo at 4, P.M. The captain said, that if there was any danger in the town, he would take us in his yawl and put us across. He walked through the town to see if there were any bills up. Finding no danger, he took us out of the hatchway,—he walked with us as far as Black Rock Ferry, giving us good advice all the way, how we should conduct ourselves through life in Canada, and we have never departed from his directions,—his counsel was good, and I have kept it.

The Fourth Try for Freedom

William Hall had seen and experienced so much terrible treatment that he was determined to gain his freedom. He got away on his fourth try, but with agonizing difficulty.

Source William Hall, from : Benjamin Drew, ed., *The Refugee: or Narratives of Fugitive Slaves in Canada Related by Themselves,* Boston, 1856, pp. 315-320.

The overseer tied me to a tree, and flogged me with the whip. Afterwards he said he would stake me down, and give me a farewell whipping, that I would always remember. While he was eating supper, I got off my shoe, and slipped off a chain and ran: I ran, I suppose, some six hundred yards: then hearing a dog, which alarmed me, I climbed a hill, where I sat down to rest. Then I heard a shouting, hallooing, for dogs to hunt me up. I tried to understand, and made out they were after me. I went through the woods to a road on a ridge. I came to a guide-board in order to read it, I pulled it up, and read it in the moonlight, and found I was going wrong-turned about and went back, travelling all night: lay by all day, travelled at night till I came where Duck River and Tennessee come together. Here I found I was wrong,—went back to a road that led down Tennessee River, the way I wanted to go. This was Monday night,- the day before they had been there for me. A colored man had told them, "God's sake to tell me not to get caught, for they would kill me:" but that I knew before. I got something to eat, and went on down the river, and travelled until Saturday night at ten, living on green corn and watermelons. Then I came to a house where an old colored man gave me a supper: another kept me with him three days. My clothes were now very dirty: I got some soap of a woman, and went to a wash-place, and washed my clothes and dried them. A heavy rain came on at daybreak, and I went down to the river for a canoe-found none-and went back for the day,-got some bread, and at night went on down the river; but there were so many roads, I could not make out how to go. I laid all day in a corn field. At night I found a canoe, 12 feet long, and travelled down the river several days, to its mouth. There I got on an island, the river being low. I took my canoe across a tongue of land,-a sandbar-into the Ohio, which I crossed into Illinois. I travelled three nights, not daring to travel days, until I came to Golconda, which I recognized by a description I had been given on a previous attempt,—for this last time when I got away was my fourth effort. I went on to three forks in the road, took the left, travelled through the night, and lay by. At two, I ventured to go on, the road not being travelled much. But it seemed to go too far west: I struck through the woods, and went on till so tired I could walk no further. I got into a tobacco-pen, and stayed till morning. Then I went through the woods, and came to where a fire had been burning-I kindled it up, roasted a lot of corn, then travelled on about three miles completely lost. I now came to a house, and revolved in my mind some hours whether to go or not, to ask. At last I ventured, and asked the road-got the information-reached Marion: got bewildered, and went wrong again, and travelled back for Golconda, -but I was set right by some children. At dark I went on, and at daybreak got to Frankfort-13 miles all night long, being weak from want of food. A few miles further on I found an old friend, who was backward about letting me in, having been troubled at night by white children. At last he let me in, and gave me some food, which I much needed. The next night he gave me as much as I could carry with me.

I went on to within five miles of Mount Vernon. At 4 A.M., I lay down, and slept till about noon. I got up and tried to walk, but every time I tried to stoop under the bushes, I would fall down. I was close to a house, but did not dare to go to it; so I laid there and was sick—vomited, and wanted water very bad. At night I was so badly off that I was obliged to go to the house for water. The man gave me some, and said," Are you a runaway? " I said, "No—I am walking away." "Where do you live?" "I live here now." "Are you a free man?" "Why should I be here, if I am not a free man?-this is a free country." "Where do you live, anyhow?" "I live here, don't you understand me?" "You are a free man, are you?" "Don't you see he is a free man, who walks in a free country?" "Show me your pass—I s'pose you've got one." "Do you suppose men need a pass in a free country? this is a free country." "I suppose you run away—a good many fugitives go through here, and do mischief." Said I, "I am doing no mischief—I am a man peaceable, going about my own business; when I am doing mischief, persecute me,—while I am peaceable, let no man trouble me." Said he, "I'll go with you to Mount Vernon." "You may go, if you have a mind to: I am going, if it is the Lord's will that I shall get there. Good evening;" and I started out of the gate. He said, "Stop!" Said I, "Man, don't bother me,-I'm sick, and do n't feel like being bothered." I kept on: he followed me,-"Stop, or I'll make you stop!" "Man, did n't I tell you I was sick, and do n't want to be bothered." I kept on,-he picked up a little maul at a wood-pile, and came with me, his little son following, to see what was going on.

He walked a mile and a quarter with me, to a neighbor of his called-there came out three men. He stated to them, "Here's a runaway going to Mount Vernon: I think it would be right to go with him." I made no reply. He said, "We'll go in with him, and if he be correct, we'll not injure him, —we'll not do him no harm, no-how." I stood consulting with myself, whether to fight or run; I concluded to run first, and fight afterward. I ran a hundred yards: one ran after me to the edge of the woods, and turned back. I sat down to rest,—say an hour. They had gone on ahead of me on horses. I took a back track, and found another road which led to Mount Vernon, which I did not reach until daybreak, although he said `t was only five miles. I hastened on very quick through town, and so got off the track again: but I found a colored friend who harbored me three days, and fulfilled the Scriptures in one sense to perfection. I was hungry, and he fed me; thirsty, and he gave me drink; weary, and he ministered to my necessities; sick, and he cared for me till I got relieved: he took me on his own beast, and carried me ten miles, and his wife gave me food for four days' travel. His name was Y——.I travelled on three nights, and every morning found myself close to a town. One was a large one. I got into it early,-I was scared, for people was stirring,-but I got through it by turning to my right, which led me thirty miles out of my way. I was trying to get to Springfield. Then I went on to Taylorville. I lay out all day, two miles out, and while there, a man came riding on horse-back within two feet of me. I thought he would see me, but he wheeled his horse, and away he went. At dark I got up and started on. It rained heavily. I went on to the town. I could discover nothing-the ground was black, the sky was cloudy. I travelled a while by the lights in the windows; at last ventured to ask the way, and got a direction for Springfield. After the rain the wind blew cold; I was chilled: I went into a calf-lot, and scared up the calves, and lay where they had been lying, to warm myself. It was dark yet. I stayed there half an hour, trying to get warm, then got up, and travelled on till daybreak. It being in a prairie, I had to travel very fast to get a place to hide myself. I came to a drain between two plantations, and got into it to hide. At sundown I went on, and reached Springfield, as near as I could guess, at 3 o'clock. I got into a stable, and lay on some boards in the loft.

When I awoke, the sun was up, and people were feeding horses in the stable. I found there was no chance to get out, without being discovered, and I went down and told them that I was a stranger, knowing no one there; that I was out until late, and so went into the stable. I asked them if there was any harm. They said "No." I thanked them and pursued my way. I walked out a little and found a friend who gave me breakfast. Then I was taken sick, and could not get a step from there for ten days: then I could walk a little, and had to start.

I took directions for Bloomington,-but the directions were wrong, and I got thirty miles out of my way again: so that when I reached Bloomington, I was too tired to go another step. I begged for a carriage, and if they had not got one, the Lord only knows what would have happened. I was conveyed to Ottawa, where I found an abolitionist who helped me to Chicago. From about the middle of August to the middle of November, I dwelt in no house except in Springfield, sick,-had no bed till I got to Bloomington. In February, I cut wood in Indiana,-I went to Wisconsin, and staid till harvest was over; then came to a particular friend, who offered me books. I had no money for books: he gave me a Testament, and gave me good instruction. I had worn out two Testaments in slavery, carrying them with me trying to get some instruction to carry me through life. "Now," said he, "square up your business, and go to the lake, for there are men here now, even here where you are living, who would betray you for half a dollar if they knew where your master is. Cross the lake: get into Canada." I thanked him for the book, which I have now; settled up and came to Canada.

Troubles on The Road

Two teenage fugitives, William and Charles Parker, ran into trouble on the way from Maryland to Pennsylvania.

Source: William Parker, "The Freedman's Story," *Atlantic Monthly* 17 (February 1866): pp. 158-159. Found in William Loren Katz, *Eyewitness, ibid.*, pp. 127-128.

The first place at which we stopped to rest was a village on the old York road, called New Market. There nothing occurred to cause us alarm; so, after taking some refreshments, we proceeded towards York; but when near Logansville, we were interrupted by three white men, one of whom, a very large man, cried—

"Hallo!"

I answered,—"Hallo to you!"

"Which way are you travelling?" he asked. We replied,—"To Little York."

"Why are you travelling so late?"

"We are not later than you are," I answered.

"Your business must be of consequence," he said.

"It is. We want to go to York to attend to it; and if you have any business, please attend to it, and don't be meddling with ours on the public highway. We have no business with you, and I am sure you have none with us."

"See here!" said he; "you are the fellows that this advertisement calls for," at the same time taking the paper out of his pocket, and reading it to us.

Sure enough, there we were, described exactly. He came closely to us, and said,—"You must go back."

I replied,—"If I must, I must, and you must take me."

"Oh, you need not make any big talk about it," he answered; "for I have taken back many a runaway, and I can take you. What's that you have in your hand?"

"A stick."

He put his hand into his pocket, as if to draw his pistol, and said,—"Come! give up your weapons."

I said again,—"Tis only a stick."

He then reached for it, when I stepped back and struck him a heavy blow on the arm. It fell as if broken; I think it was. Then he turned and ran, and I after him. As he ran, he would look back over his shoulder, see me coming, and then run faster, and haloo with all his might. I could not catch him, and it seemed, that, the longer he ran, the faster he went. The other two took to their heels at the first alarm,— thus illustrating the valor of the [Southern] chivalry!

At last I gave up the chase. The whole neighborhood by that time was aroused, and we thought best to retrace our steps to the place whence we started. Then we took a round-about course until we reached the railroad, along which we travelled. For a long distance there was unusual stir and commotion. Every house was lighted up; and we heard people talking and horses galloping this way and that way, with other evidences of unusual excitement. This was between one and two o'clock in the morning.

Those Who Helped

Of the thousands of fugitives who escaped bondage, some made their way to freedom entirely on their own. A number of them were given shelter by Seminole Indians and by communities of freed African Americans. Others were helped to travel north by the conductors and station managers of the Underground Railroad, many of whom were African Americans.

African-American churches were active in supporting the railroad. The first black church in Boston, the African Meeting House, was built by free black people in 1806. The building served as a church, a school, a place for celebrations, and as a gathering place for abolitionists. The second black church in Boston, the Twelfth Baptist Church, became known as the "fugitive slave church" because so many had benefited from the congregation's efforts.

As early as 1688, Pennsylvania Quakers opposed slavery on religious grounds. (See Wim Coleman, ed., American Quakers, *Discovery Enterprises, 1998.) Many Quakers were active helpers on the Underground Railroad.*

In the northern states, a growing number of well-known people, black and white, identified themselves as Abolitionists. William Lloyd Garrison, John Greenleaf Whittier, James Russell Lowell, and Frederick Douglass were among them.

There was no general agreement among Abolitionists. Some were for immediate abolition of slavery, others for more gradual change. Some favored creating states in Africa for free African Americans. Some favored political action, others called for personal action—sometimes of a violent nature. Some did not believe in aiding runaway slaves, but many other Abolitionists were quite active in the Underground Railroad.

Moses Leads the Way

Harriet Tubman

Harriet Tubman (1820–1913) escaped slavery and became one of the leading Abolitionists. She soon became one of the most active conductors on the Underground Railroad. Even though large rewards were offered for her capture, Tubman acted again and again, helping more than 300 other slaves escape. She was said to maintain military discipline, even to force some weary travelers along with a loaded revolver.

During the Civil War, Tubman was a nurse, laundress, and a spy. (See Phyllis Rabin Emert, ed., Women in the Civil War: Warriors, Patriots, Nurses, and Spies, *Discovery Enterprises, 1995.) The following account was published while Tubman was involved in her Underground Railroad activities.*

Source: *The Freedmen's Record*, Vol. 1, No. 3, Boston, March, 1865, pp. 34-38.

One of the teachers lately commissioned by the New-England Freedmen's Aid Society is probably the most remarkable woman of this age. That is to say, she has performed more wonderful deeds by the native power of her own spirit against adverse circumstances than any other. She is well known to many by the various names which her eventful life has given her; Harriet Garrison, Gen. Tubman, &c.; but among the slaves she is universally known by her well-earned title of *Moses*,—Moses the deliverer. She is a rare instance, in the midst of high civilization and intellectual culture, of a being of great native powers, working powerfully, and to beneficient ends, entirely unaided by schools or books.

Her maiden name was Araminta Ross. She is the granddaughter of a native African, and has not a drop of white blood in her veins. She was born in 1820 or 1821, on the Eastern Shore of Maryland. Her parents were slaves, but married and faithful to each other, and the family affection is very strong. She claims that she was legally freed by a will of her first master, but his wishes were not carried into effect. . . .

When quite young she lived with a very pious mistress; but the slaveholder's religion did not prevent her from whipping the young girl for every slight or fancied fault. Araminta found that this was usually a morning exercise; so she prepared for it by putting on all the thick clothes she could procure to protect her skin. She made sufficient outcry, however, to convince her mistress that her blows had full effect; and in the afternoon she would take off her wrappings, and dress as well as she could. . . .

. . . She was married about 1844 to a free colored man named John Tubman, but never had any children. Owing to changes in her owner's family, it was determined to sell her and some other slaves; but [a blow to the head had injured her and] a purchaser was not easily found. At length she became convinced that she would soon be carried away, and she decided to escape. Her brothers did not agree with her plans; and she walked off alone, following the guidance of the brooks, which she had observed to run North. The evening before she left, she wished very much to bid her companions farewell, but was afraid of being betrayed, if any one knew of her intentions; so she passed through the street singing,—

"Good bye, I'm going to leave you,

Good bye, I'll meet you in the kingdom,"—and similar snatches of Methodist songs. . . .

[After escaping across the Mason-Dixon Line into a free state, Tubman went back for her husband but he had taken another wife and refused to join her.]

[B]ut finally she thought . . . "if he could do without her, she could without him," and so "he dropped out of her heart," and she determined to give her life to brave deeds. Thus all personal aims died out of her heart; and with her simple brave motto, "I can't die but once," she began the work which has made her Moses,—the deliverer of her people. Seven or eight times she has returned to the neighborhood of her former home, always at the risk of death in the most terrible forms, and each time has brought away a company of fugitive slaves, and led them safely to the free States, or to Canada. Every time she went, the dangers increased. In 1857 she brought away her old parents, and, as they were too feeble to walk, she was obliged to hire a wagon, which added greatly to the perils of the journey. In 1860 she went for the last time, and among her troop was an infant whom they were obliged to keep stupefied with laudanum to prevent its outcries. This was at the period of great excitement, and Moses was not safe even in New-York State; but her anxious friends insisted upon her taking refuge in Canada. So various and interesting are the incidents of the journeys, that we know not how to select from them. She has shown in them all the characteristics of a great leader: courage, foresight, prudence, self-control, ingenuity, subtle perception, command over others' minds.

A clergyman once said, that her stories convinced you of their truth by their simplicity as do the gospel narratives. She never went to the South to bring away fugitives without being provided with money; money for the most part earned by drudgery in the kitchen, until within the last few years, when friends have aided her. She had to leave her sister's two orphan children in slavery the last time, for the want of thirty dollars. Thirty pieces of silver; an embroidered handkerchief or a silk dress to one, or the price of freedom to two orphan children to another! She would never allow more to join her than she could properly care for, though she often gave others directions by which they succeeded in escaping. She always came in the winter when the nights are long and dark, and people who have homes stay in them. She was never seen on the plantation herself; but appointed a rendezvous for her company eight or ten miles distant, so that if they were discovered at the first start she was not compromised. She started on Saturday night; the slaves at that time being allowed to go away from home to visit their friends,—so that they would not be missed until Monday morning. Even then they were supposed to have loitered on the way, and it would often be late on Monday afternoon before the flight would be certainly known. If by any further delay the advertisement was not sent out before Tuesday morning, she felt secure of keeping ahead of it; but if it were, it required all her ingenuity to escape. She resorted to various devices, she had confidential friends all along the road. She would hire a man to follow the one who put up the notices, and take them down as soon as his back was turned. She crossed creeks on railroad bridges by night, she hid her company in the woods while she herself not being advertised went into the towns in search of information. If met on the road, her face was always to the south, and she was always a very respectable looking darkey, not at all a poor fugitive. . . .

The expedition was governed by the strictest rules. If any man gave out, he must be shot. "Would you really do that?" she was asked. "Yes," she replied, "if he was weak enough to give out, he'd be weak enough to betray us all, and all who had helped us; and do you think I'd let so many die just for one coward man." "Did you ever have to shoot any one?" she was asked. "One time," she said, a man gave out the second night; his feet were sore and swollen, he couldn't go any further; he'd rather go back and die, if he must." They tried all arguments in vain, bathed his feet, tried to strengthen him, but it was of no use, he would go back. Then she said, "I told the boys to get their guns ready, and shoot him. They'd have done it in a minute; but when he heard that, he jumped right up and went on as well as any body." She can tell the time by the stars, and find her way by natural signs as well as any hunter; and yet she scarcely knows of the existence of England or any other foreign country. . . .

Her efforts were not confined to the escape of slaves. She conducted them to Canada, watched over their welfare, collected clothing, organized them into societies, and was always occupied with plans for their benefit. . . .

. . . Her personal appearance is very peculiar. She is thoroughly negro, and very plain. She has needed disguise so often, that she seems to have command over her face, and can banish all expression from her features, and look so stupid that nobody would suspect her of knowing enough to be dangerous; . . .

Levi Coffin's Railroad Station

Levi Coffin was born and raised a Quaker in North Carolina, where he saw slavery in action. In the mid-1820s, he moved to Newport, Indiana, where he and his wife, Catharine, became legendary for the help they gave to former slaves traveling on the Underground Railroad. Coffin was so dedicated to helping fugitive slaves gain their freedom that he was often referred to at the "President" of the Underground Railroad. A brief excerpt from his journal follows.

Source: Levi Coffin, *Reminiscences of Levi Coffin* (Cincinnati, 1876), pp. 10-12.

. . . I found that we were on a line of the U.G.R.R. [Underground Railroad]. Fugitives often passed through that place, and generally stopped among the colored people. . . . I learned that the fugitive slaves who took refuge with these people were often pursued and captured, the colored people not being very skillful in concealing them, or shrewd in making arrangements to forward them to Canada. . . . I was willing to receive and aid as many fugitives as were disposed to come to my house. . . .

Coffin's beds concealed a small room behind this short door.

... In the winter of 1826-27, fugitives began to come to our house, and as it became more widely known on different routes that the slaves fleeing from bondage would find a welcome and shelter at our house, and be forwarded safely on their journey, the number increased. Friends in the neighborhood, who had formerly stood aloof from the work, fearful of the penalty of the law, were encouraged to engage in it when they saw the fearless manner in which I acted, and the success that attended my efforts. . . .

... the Underground Railroad business increased as time advanced, and it was attended with heavy expenses, which I could not have borne had not my affairs been prosperous. I found it necessary to keep a team and a wagon always at command, to convey the fugitive slaves on their journey. Sometimes, when we had large companies, one or two other teams and wagons were required. These journeys had to be made at night, often through deep mud and bad roads, and along by ways that were seldom traveled. Every precaution to evade pursuit had to be used, as the hunters were often on the track, and sometimes ahead of the slaves. . . .

I soon became extensively known to the friends of the slaves, at different points on the Ohio River, where fugitives generally crossed, and to those northward of us on the various routes leading to Canada. . . . Seldom a week passed without our receiving passengers. . . .

Epilogue

Even those who succeeded in escaping slavery still had many problems to face, as Frederick Douglass explained.

Source: Frederick Douglass, *Narrative of the Life of Frederick Douglass, An American Slave, Written by Himself.* Boston: 1845; New York: Doubleday & Co., 1963, p. 106.

I have been frequently asked how I felt when I found myself in a free State. I have never been able to answer the question with any satisfaction to myself. It was a moment of the highest excitement I ever experienced. . . . I felt like one who had escaped a den of hungry lions. This state of mind, however, very soon subsided; and I was again seized with a feeling of great insecurity and loneliness. I was yet liable to be taken back, and subjected to all the tortures of slavery. This in itself was enough to damp the ardor of my enthusiasm. But the loneliness overcame me. There I was in the midst of thousands, and yet a perfect stranger; without home and without friends, in the midst of thousands of my own brethren—children of a common Father, and yet I dared not to unfold to any one of them my sad condition. I was afraid to speak to any one for fear of speaking to the wrong one, and thereby falling into the hands of money-loving kidnappers. . . .

On December 18, 1865, the Thirteenth Amendment to the Constitution was ratified, permanently abolishing slavery. After that, the Underground Railroad could close down, but the triumphant African-Americans would still face many cultural problems. Frederick Douglass was worried about the future—but even he couldn't have guessed the challenges that lay ahead.

Suggested Further Reading

Badt, Karin Luisa. *The Underground Railroad – A Reproducible Play with Music*. Carlisle, MA: Discovery Enterprises, Ltd., 1996.

Chittenden, Elizabeth F. *Profiles in Black and White – Stories of Men and Women Who Fought Against Slavery*. New York: Charles Scribner's Sons, 1973.

Cosner, Sharon. *The Underground Railroad*. New York: Franklin Watts, 1991.

Freedman, Florence B. *Two Tickets to Freedom – The True Story of Ellen and William Craft, Fugitive Slaves*. New York: Peter Bedrick Books,1971.

Hamilton, Virginia. *Anthony Burns: The Defeat and Triumph of a Fugitive Slave*. New York: Alfred A. Knopf, 1988.

Khan, Lurey. *One Day, Levin . . . He Be Free – William Still and the Underground Railroad*. New York: E.P. Dutton & Co., Inc., 1972.

Petry, Ann. *Harriet Tubman – Conductor on the Underground Railroad*. New York: Simon & Schuster, 1955.

Russell, Sharman Apt. *Frederick Douglass – Abolitionist Editor*. New York: Chelsea House Publishers, 1988.

Scott, John Anthony. *Hard Trials on My Way: Slavery and the Struggle Against It, 1800-1860*. New York: Alfred A. Knopf, Inc., 1974.

Taylor, M.W. *Harriet Tubman –Antislavery Activist*. New York: Chelsea House Publishers, 1991.

Tobin, Jacqueline L., Raymond G., Phd. Dobard, Cuesta Ray Benberry. *Hidden in Plain View: A secret story of quilts & the underground railroad*. October 1997.